BARBECUES

Lakeland and ACP Magazines Ltd hereby exclude all liability to the extent permitted by law for any errors or omission in this book and for any loss, damage or expense (whether direct or indirect) suffered by a third party relying on any information contained in this book.

This book was created in 2013 for Lakeland by AWW Books, an imprint of Octopus Publishing Group Ltd, based on materials licensed to it by ACP Magazines Ltd, a division of Nine Entertainment Co.

54 Park St, Sydney
GPO Box 4088, Sydney, NSW 2001.
phone (02) 9282 8618; fax (02) 9126 3702
acpbooks@acpmagazines.com.au;
www.acpbooks.com.au

OCTOPUS PUBLISHING GROUP
Design – Chris Bell
Food Director – Pamela Clark

Published for Lakeland in the United Kingdom by Octopus Publishing Group Limited

Endeavour House
189 Shaftesbury Avenue
London WC2H 8JY
United Kingdom
phone + 44 (0) 207 632 5400;
fax + 44 (0) 207 632 5405
aww@octopusbooks.co.uk;
www.octopusbooks.co.uk
www.australian-womens-weekly.com

Printed and bound in China

A catalogue record for this book is available from the British Library.

ISBN 978-1-907428-88-3

The Department of Health advises that eggs should not be consumed raw. This book contains some dishes made with raw or lightly cooked eggs. It is prudent for vulnerable people such as pregnant and nursing mothers, invalids, the elderly, babies and young children to avoid uncooked or lightly cooked dishes made with eggs. Once prepared, these dishes should be kept refrigerated and used promptly.

This book also includes dishes made with nuts and nut derivatives. It is advisable for those with known allergic reactions to nuts and nut derivatives and those who may be potentially vulnerable to these allergies, such as pregnant and nursing mothers, invalids, the elderly, babies and children to avoid dishes made with nuts and nut oils. It is also prudent to check the labels of pre-prepared ingredients for the possible inclusion of nut derivatives.

Some of the recipes in this book have appeared in other publications.

BARBECUES

Nothing beats a barbecue on a summer's day, so light the charcoal, grab the tongs and enjoy over 60 great recipes for everything from juicy burgers and kebabs to sumptuous salads and tempting vegetarian options.

One of an exciting new series of cookbooks from Lakeland, *Barbecues* is packed with delicious colour photos plus expert hints, tips and techniques for beginners and experienced cooks alike.

With every recipe triple-tested® for perfect results, these excellent cookbooks are sure to become some of the best-loved on your kitchen bookshelf. To discover the rest of the range, together with our unrivalled selection of creative kitchenware, visit one of our friendly Lakeland stores or shop online at www.lakeland.co.uk.

CONTENTS

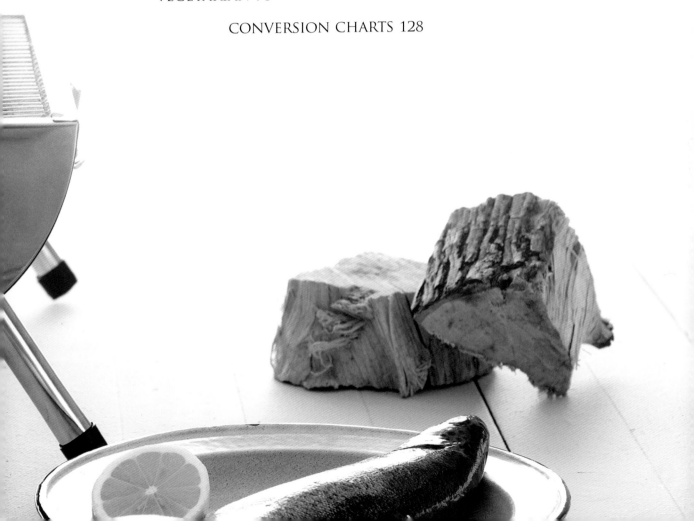

BARBECUE BASICS

Barbecuing is an indispensable part of summer life and offers a casual, relaxed way of cooking for family and friends.

CHOOSING A BARBECUE

When it comes to deciding which barbecue is best for you, consider whether you want the option of cooking joints of meat or whole birds using a barbecue with indirect heat or whether you'll use it only for cooking things like sausages, burgers and steaks over a direct heat. A covered or kettle barbecue – one with a domed lid – is the most useful because you can use it as an oven with the lid closed or as a traditional barbecue with the lid open.

Other considerations are size – think about how many people are you likely to be cooking for, whether you need it to be easily portable and which fuel you want to use.

Gas or charcoal?

Gas is a comfortable compromise between convenience and flavour. It is clean, easy to use and heats the barbecue quickly. Charcoal gives food a wonderful smoky flavour but can be hard to get

going and a charcoal barbecue takes a long time to heat up.

FIRE IT UP

Just before heating the barbecue, brush or spray the barbecue grill with melted butter or oil. Around 10–15 minutes should be enough to heat a gas barbecue but a charcoal barbecue can take around 30 minutes and up an

hour to be properly hot. Allow the coals to burn down until they are covered with grey ash and spread them out before you start cooking. Don't start cooking until the firelighters are burning or your food will taste of kerosene.

If using a kettle barbecue, set up the coals for direct or indirect heat, as required, after the coals are hot. For indirect heat, move coals to the outside edges of the barbecue and cook food in the centre. Use a disposable foil baking tray nestled in the coals to catch drips.

Ready to cook?

Ensure the barbecue is at the temperature required by a recipe before adding the food. A good heat test is to see how long you can hold your hand just above the grill. If the fire is very hot, you can hold your hand in place for 1 second or less, 3 seconds for a medium-hot barbecue and 5 seconds for a low to medium heat.

DIRECT HEAT COOKING

Sausages

Don't prick sausages before cooking them as this simply allows the juices to drain out, leaving your sausages dry and tasteless. For the best results, sausages should cook for a long time over a low heat; if they look like they are about to burst, move them to a cooler part of the barbecue.

Steaks & burgers

For nicely char-marked steaks and burgers, grill them for a few minutes without moving and turn once only so that the marks will be clearly defined.

Basting

Baste food frequently with melted butter or oil or with a marinade or sauce, if specified in the recipe.

Cooking times

The times suggested in this book are a guide only, so test before the cooking time is complete. Poultry

USEFUL EQUIPMENT

- Long-handled tongs
- Long-handled fork
- Long-handled spatula
- Basting brush
- Fish grill
- Disposable foil baking trays
- Bamboo skewers
- Stiff wire brush for cleaning

INDIRECT HEAT COOKING

Indirect heat is great for cooking large joints of meat or a whole chicken, which is really useful if you're feeding a crowd. Follow the manufacturer's guidelines to heat the barbecue to the required temperature.

Cooking

Place the meat or poultry on a wire rack in a disposable foil baking tray and baste frequently to keep it moist. Once cooked, meat or poultry should be rested, covered loosely with foil on a warm plate. This allows the juices to settle, resulting in more tender meat.

Meat

Test to see if meat is cooked by inserting a skewer into it. For rare meat the juices should run red; if the juices are pink the meat is medium-rare and, if they are clear, the meat is well done.

Poultry

Poultry is cooked only when the juices run without a trace of pink when a skewer is inserted into the fleshy part of bird. Protect wings or legs from burning by loosely covering them with aluminium foil.

Fish

Cooking a whole fish or large pieces of fish is easiest if you use a fish grill. This keeps the fish intact and allows you to flip it over easily. Slash the sides of the fish a few times before placing it on the barbecue.

Fish is cooked when a skewer is inserted easily into its flesh. Remember to take it off the barbecue just before it is completely cooked.

CLEANING THE BARBECUE

All barbecues should be cleaned after use and it is easiest to do this while it the barbecue still warm but not hot. Scrub the grill and hotplates (if your barbecue has them) with a stiff wire brush and cold water (no detergent). Wipe dry with newspaper or an old towel. Allow to cool and lightly spray or brush with vegetable oil to prevent rusting.

must always be cooked through before serving – test to see if it is cooked by inserting a skewer into it; any juices should be completely clear. However, don't cut into meat to test for doneness, as this will release all the juices that make it tender and moist. Instead, press on the surface of the meat with your tongs. Rare meat will be soft to the touch, medium will be firm and well-done meat will feel very firm to the touch.

Seafood

Seafood should be removed from the barbecue while it is still a shade underdone; its own heat will finish the cooking by the time it is served. Fillets of fish are too delicate to cook directly on a barbecue and should either be wrapped in, or cooked on, aluminium foil. Baste once or twice and cook for about 4 minutes for fillets and 7 minutes for thick steaks.

> **HERBS**
>
> When you prune your bay tree or rosemary bush, save the clippings and toss them on the fire before cooking. The flavours of the herbs with permeate the food and add delicious extra flavour.

MEAT

CHILLI-RUBBED HICKORY-SMOKED RIB-EYE STEAKS

1 tablespoon finely grated
  lemon rind
2 teaspoons chilli powder
2 teaspoons dried thyme
1 teaspoon smoked paprika
2 tablespoons olive oil
2 cloves garlic, crushed
4 x 200g beef rib-eye steaks
100g hickory smoking chips
500ml water

1 Combine rind, chilli, thyme, paprika, oil and garlic in large bowl; add beef, turn to coat in mixture. Cover; refrigerate 3 hours or overnight.
2 Soak chips in the water in medium bowl; stand 3 hours or overnight.
3 Place drained chips in smoke box alongside beef on grill plate. Cook beef in covered barbecue, using indirect heat, following manufacturer's directions, about 10 minutes or until cooked as desired.

prep + cook time 20 minutes + refrigeration time
serves 4
nutritional count per serving 27.3g total fat (8.9g saturated fat); 1726kJ (413 cal); 0.4g carbohydrate; 41.1g protein; 0.7g fibre
tip You need smoking chips and a smoke box for this recipe. Smoke boxes and smoking chips are available at most big garden centres and online.

SCOTCH FILLET STEAKS WITH ONION & GARLIC MUSHROOMS

125ml dry red wine
2 tablespoons coarsely chopped
    fresh basil
2 cloves garlic, crushed
6 x 200g beef scotch fillet steaks
20g butter
6 medium red onions (1kg),
    sliced thinly
75g brown sugar
60ml red wine vinegar
6 large flat mushrooms (840g)
2 tablespoons olive oil
1 clove garlic, crushed, extra
1 teaspoon lemon pepper

1 Combine wine, basil and garlic in large bowl; add beef, turn to coat in mixture. Cover; refrigerate 3 hours or overnight.
2 Melt butter in large frying pan; cook onion, stirring, until soft and browned lightly. Stir in sugar and vinegar; cook, stirring constantly, about 20 minutes or until onion is well browned and mixture has thickened.
3 Brush mushrooms with combined oil, extra garlic and lemon pepper; cook on heated oiled barbecue until tender.
4 Drain beef; discard marinade. Cook beef on heated oiled barbecue until cooked as desired.
5 Top each piece of beef with a mushroom and a little caramelised onion.

prep + cook time 1 hour 15 minutes + refrigeration time
serves 6
nutritional count per serving
21g total fat (7.7g saturated fat); 1977kJ (473 cal); 21.4g carbohydrate; 44.8g protein; 2.5g fibre

BEEF BURGERS WITH AUBERGINE & HUMMUS

600g minced beef
2 teaspoons ground cumin
2 cloves garlic, crushed
3 tablespoons finely chopped
  fresh coriander
1 large aubergine (240g), sliced
  thickly
3 medium plum tomatoes (225g),
  sliced thickly
1 medium brown onion (150g),
  sliced thinly
8 slices sourdough bread (560g)
130g hummus
2 teaspoons lemon juice
1 teaspoon olive oil
100g rocket

1 Combine beef, cumin, garlic and coriander in medium bowl; shape mixture into four patties.
2 Cook patties, aubergine, tomato and onion, in batches, on heated oiled barbecue until patties are cooked through and aubergine is tender.
3 Grill bread on same cleaned barbecue until browned on both sides.
4 Meanwhile, combine hummus, juice and oil in small bowl.
5 Sandwich rocket, aubergine, patties, tomato, hummus and onion between bread slices.

prep + cook time 25 minutes
serves 4
nutritional count per serving
21.2g total fat (6.2g saturated fat); 2913kJ (697 cal); 71.6g carbohydrate; 48.1g protein; 12.6g fibre

PEPPERED BEEF ROAST

2 teaspoons paprika
2 teaspoons ground black pepper
1 tablespoon coarse ground
  black pepper
1 teaspoon ground cardamom
1kg boneless beef rib-eye roast
180ml japanese soy sauce
125ml cider vinegar
2 teaspoons tomato paste
1 clove garlic, crushed

1 Combine spices in small bowl; rub all over beef. Combine beef with remaining ingredients in shallow bowl. Cover; refrigerate 3 hours or overnight, turning occasionally.
2 Heat covered barbecue to 180°C/350°F. Place roast in disposable baking dish; brush with marinade. Cook, using indirect heat, about 1½ hours. Remove roast from barbecue; cover, stand 5 minutes before slicing.

prep + cook time 1 hour 45 minutes + refrigeration time
serves 4
nutritional count per serving
15.5g total fat (6.8g saturated fat); 1542kJ (369 cal); 1.6g carbohydrate; 53.7g protein; 0.2g fibre

BEEF RIBS WITH MAPLE & SHERRY GLAZE

2 tablespoons finely chopped
   fresh lemongrass
3 strips fresh lime peel, chopped
   finely
1 teaspoon sea salt
2cm piece fresh ginger (10g),
   grated
2 cloves garlic, quartered
6 racks beef thin ribs (900g)
180ml sweet sherry
110g dark brown sugar
125ml maple syrup
2 tablespoons sesame oil
1 tablespoon five-spice powder

1 Pound lemongrass, lime peel, salt, ginger and garlic in mortar and pestle until fragrant.
2 Combine lemongrass mixture with remaining ingredients in large bowl. Cover, refrigerate 3 hours or overnight.
3 Remove ribs from marinade; transfer marinade to medium saucepan.
4 Cook ribs on heated oiled barbecue until browned on both sides and cooked as desired; season to taste. Remove ribs from barbecue; cover, stand 5 minutes.
5 Meanwhile, bring marinade to the boil; reduce heat, simmer, uncovered, about 10 minutes or until thickened.
6 Serve ribs drizzled with the marinade.

prep + cook time 30 minutes + refrigeration time
serves 6
nutritional count per serving
13.3g total fat (3.9g saturated fat); 1634kJ (391 cal); 39.9g carbohydrate; 22.5g protein; 0.2g fibre

FENNEL VEAL CHOPS
WITH GARLIC MUSTARD BUTTER

2 teaspoons fennel seeds
1 teaspoon sea salt
½ teaspoon coarse ground black
   pepper
2 tablespoons olive oil
4 x 200g veal chops
4 flat mushrooms (320g)
80g butter, softened
1 tablespoon coarsely chopped
   fresh flat-leaf parsley
1 clove garlic, crushed
1 tablespoon wholegrain mustard
80g rocket

1 Using mortar and pestle, coarsely crush combined seeds, salt and pepper; stir in oil. Rub mixture over veal.
2 Cook veal and mushrooms on heated oiled barbecue until browned both sides and cooked as desired.
3 Meanwhile, combine butter, parsley, garlic and mustard in small bowl.
4 Divide rocket among serving plates; top each with mushroom, veal then butter mixture.

prep + cook time 25 minutes
serves 4
nutritional count per serving
29.7g total fat (13.2g saturated fat); 1831kJ (438 cal); 2.1g carbohydrate; 39.9g protein; 2.7g fibre

CINNAMON MARMALADE PORK

2 tablespoons orange marmalade
2 tablespoons olive oil
¼ teaspoon ground cinnamon
4 x 125g pork loin medallions
125g fine green beans, trimmed
2 medium oranges (480g)
2 red grapefruit (700g)
1 tablespoon white wine vinegar
350g bunch watercress, trimmed

1 Whisk marmalade, half the oil and the cinnamon in large bowl until smooth. Add pork; turn to coat in marmalade mixture.
2 Cook pork on heated oiled barbecue until browned on both sides and cooked through. Remove pork from barbecue; cover, stand 5 minutes.
3 Meanwhile, boil, steam or microwave green beans until tender; drain. Rinse under cold water; drain.
4 Segment the oranges and grapefruit, separately, over small bowl; reserve 1 tablespoon orange juice.
5 Whisk reserved juice, remaining oil and vinegar in large bowl. Add orange and grapefruit segments, beans and watercress; toss gently.
6 Serve pork with salad.

prep + cook time 45 minutes
serves 4
nutritional count per serving
12.6g total fat (2.2g saturated fat); 1488kJ (356 cal); 22.5g carbohydrate; 34.2g protein; 6.7g fibre

PORK & PROSCIUTTO KEBABS

650g pork fillets
2 tablespoons chopped fresh
   sage
8 slices prosciutto

1 Cut pork fillets into 2.5cm pieces. Combine fillets and sage in medium bowl.

2 Cut prosciutto in half lengthways. Wrap half the fillets in prosciutto; thread plain fillets alternately with prosciutto-wrapped fillets onto 8 skewers.

3 Cook skewers on heated oiled barbecue until browned on both sides and cooked through.

prep + cook time 20 minutes
makes 8
nutritional count per kebab
0.7g total fat (0.2g saturated fat); 93kJ (22 cal); 0g carbohydrate; 4.1g protein; 0g fibre
tip You need 8 skewers for this recipe. If you use bamboo skewers, soak them in cold water for at least 1 hour before using to prevent them splintering and scorching during cooking.

PORK RIBS WITH STICKY BARBECUE SAUCE

1.75kg american-style pork
  spare ribs
250ml tomato ketchup
110g light brown sugar
2 cloves garlic, crushed
2 tablespoons worcestershire
  sauce
1 tablespoon cider vinegar
2 teaspoons smoked paprika

1 Bring large saucepan of water to the boil. Reduce heat to medium. Simmer ribs, covered, about 40 minutes or until tender. Drain.

2 Combine remaining ingredients in medium bowl with ribs.

3 Cook ribs on heated oiled barbecue about 15 minutes, basting with remaining marinade every 5 minutes.

4 Cut ribs into serving-sized portions.

prep + cook time 45 minutes
serves 4
nutritional count per serving
15g total fat (5.7g saturated fat); 2307kJ (552 cal); 44.7g carbohydrate; 60.2g protein; 1.6g fibre

SAUSAGES WITH TOMATO RELISH

1 tablespoon olive oil
1 clove garlic, crushed
1 medium brown onion (150g),
  chopped coarsely
2 large tomatoes (500g), chopped
  coarsely
1 tablespoon balsamic vinegar
1 teaspoon brown sugar
1 tablespoon torn fresh basil
  leaves
8 thin pork sausages

1 Heat oil in small saucepan, add garlic and onion; cook, stirring, until browned lightly. Add tomato, vinegar and sugar; simmer, uncovered, stirring occasionally, about 20 minutes or until mixture is reduced by half. Just before serving, stir through basil.
2 Meanwhile, cook sausages on heated oiled barbecue until browned and cooked through.
3 Serve sausages with warm tomato relish. Sprinkle with extra basil leaves, if desired.

prep + cook time 45 minutes
serves 4
nutritional count per serving
30.5g total fat (11.1g saturated fat); 1576kJ (377 cal); 9g carbohydrate; 15.8g protein; 3.6g fibre

LAMB CHOPS WITH
SUN-DRIED TOMATO PESTO

6 lamb chump chops (660g)
125ml lemon juice
125ml dry white wine
2 cloves garlic, crushed

sun-dried tomato pesto
150g drained sun-dried
  tomatoes in oil
125ml olive oil
80g roasted pine nuts
25g grated parmesan cheese
2 tablespoons lemon juice
2 cloves garlic, crushed

1 Trim fat from lamb. Place lamb in shallow dish; pour over combined juice, wine and garlic. Cover; refrigerate 3 hours or overnight.
2 Make sun-dried tomato pesto.
3 Drain lamb; discard marinade. Cook lamb on heated oiled barbecue until cooked as desired.
4 Serve lamb with sun-dried tomato pesto.

sun-dried tomato pesto Blend or process ingredients until combined.

prep + cook time 30 minutes + refrigeration time
serves 6
nutritional count per serving 41g total fat (8.7g saturated fat); 2182kJ (522 cal); 10.1g carbohydrate; 23.5g protein; 4.6g fibre

LAMB YAKITORI

125ml japanese soy sauce
125ml sake
60ml mirin
2 tablespoons granulated sugar
500g diced lamb
1 medium carrot (120g), sliced thinly
6 spring onions, cut into 3cm lengths

1 Bring sauce, sake, mirin and sugar to the boil in small saucepan. Reduce heat; simmer, uncovered, until sauce reduces by a third. Cool 10 minutes.
2 Meanwhile, thread lamb, carrot and onion, alternately, onto skewers.
3 Cook skewers on heated oiled barbecue brushing with half the sauce occasionally, until browned all over and cooked as desired. Serve yakitori with remaining sauce.

prep + cook time 40 minutes
makes 8
nutritional count per serving
11.1g total fat (5g saturated fat); 1229kJ (294 cal); 12.1g carbohydrate; 28.4g protein; 1.1g fibre
tip You need 8 bamboo skewers for this recipe. Soak them in cold water for at least 1 hour before using to prevent them splintering and scorching during cooking.

LAMB BURGERS WITH BEETROOT RELISH & YOGURT

500g minced lamb
1 small brown onion (80g),
  chopped finely
2 cloves garlic, crushed
1 teaspoon ground cumin
1 egg, beaten lightly
210g natural yogurt
½ teaspoon ground cumin, extra
1 tablespoon finely chopped
  fresh mint
1 large ciabatta loaf
50g rocket leaves

beetroot relish
80ml water
4 medium beetroot (700g),
  trimmed, grated coarsely
1 small brown onion (80g),
  chopped finely
110g granulated sugar
160ml cider vinegar

1 Make beetroot relish.
2 Meanwhile, combine lamb, onion, garlic, cumin and egg in medium bowl; shape mixture into four patties.
3 Cook patties on heated oiled barbecue until cooked through. Cover to keep warm.
4 Combine yogurt, extra cumin and mint in small bowl.
5 Cut bread into quarters; halve quarters horizontally. Toast bread on heated oiled barbecue.
6 Sandwich rocket, patties, yogurt mixture and relish between toast pieces.

beetroot relish Combine the water, beetroot and onion in large frying pan; cook, covered, about 15 minutes or until beetroot is tender. Stir in sugar and vinegar; cook, covered, stirring occasionally, 20 minutes. Uncover; cook, stirring occasionally, about 10 minutes or until liquid evaporates.

prep + cook time 1 hour 15 minutes
serves 4
nutritional count per serving 22g total fat (7.9g saturated fat); 3173kJ (759 cal); 95.9g carbohydrate; 43.6g protein; 8.6g fibre
tip Beetroot relish will keep, covered and refrigerated, for up to three days.

LAMB RACKS WITH PEPPER PESTO, ASPARAGUS & CORN

300g drained roasted red
  peppers
40g pine nuts, roasted
60ml olive oil
3 tablespoons coarsely chopped
  fresh basil leaves
1 fresh long red chilli, chopped
  coarsely
1 tablespoon palm sugar
4 x 6-cutlet french-trimmed lamb
  racks (1.5kg)
2 large corn cobs (800g), trimmed
500g asparagus, trimmed
3 shallots (75g), sliced thinly
2 tablespoons finely chopped
  fresh flat-leaf parsley
1 tablespoon lime juice
½ teaspoon chilli powder

1 Blend or process pepper, nuts, oil, basil, chopped chilli and sugar until smooth; season. Combine half the paste with lamb racks in large shallow bowl; cover, refrigerate 3 hours or overnight.
2 Place lamb in deep disposable baking dish; cook in covered barbecue using indirect heat about 15 minutes. Cover lamb, stand 10 minutes before cutting into serving-sized portions.
3 Meanwhile, boil, steam or microwave corn until tender; drain. When cool enough to handle, cut corn kernels, in small slabs, from cobs.
4 Cook asparagus on heated oiled barbecue until tender. Combine shallots, parsley, juice and powdered chilli in small bowl; drizzle over asparagus and corn.
5 Serve lamb with corn, asparagus and reserved paste thinned with a little hot water, if necessary.

prep + cook time 45 minutes + refrigeration time
serves 8
nutritional count per serving 17.8g total fat (4.1g saturated fat); 1359kJ (325 cal); 16.7g carbohydrate; 22g protein; 5.3g fibre

LAMB CUTLETS WITH TOMATO & CORIANDER SALSA

1 teaspoon ground coriander
½ teaspoon ground cumin
2 cloves garlic, crushed
1 teaspoon olive oil
2 tablespoons finely grated lemon rind
60ml lemon juice
12 french-trimmed lamb cutlets (600g)

tomato & coriander salsa
2 small tomatoes (180g), chopped finely
1 small red onion (80g), chopped finely
1 clove garlic, crushed
1 tablespoon red wine vinegar
1 tablespoon finely chopped fresh coriander

1 Combine spices, garlic, oil, rind and juice in small bowl; rub mixture over cutlets, stand 10 minutes.
2 Cook cutlets on heated oiled barbecue until cooked as desired.
3 Meanwhile, make tomato & coriander salsa. Serve cutlets topped with salsa.

tomato & coriander salsa
Combine ingredients in small bowl; season to taste.

prep + cook time 25 minutes
serves 4
nutritional count per serving
8.7g total fat (3.6g saturated fat); 698kJ (167 cal); 2.7g carbohydrate; 17.9g protein; 1.4g fibre

POULTRY

CHICKEN PARCELS

600g salad potatoes, halved
   lengthways
4 x 155g chicken breast fillets
120g ricotta cheese
150g baby spinach leaves
50g drained semi-dried tomatoes
   in oil
100g wafer-thin ham
1 clove garlic, crushed
1 tablespoon fresh lemon thyme
   leaves
1 tablespoon olive oil
1 tablespoon balsamic vinegar
½ cucumber (130g), halved
   lengthways, deseeded, sliced
   thinly
1 small red onion (80g), sliced
   thinly

1 Boil, steam or microwave potatoes until tender; drain.

2 Meanwhile, cut chicken breasts in half horizontally without cutting all the way through; open chicken out flat. Layer cheese, then about a quarter of the spinach, the tomatoes and ham over half of each chicken breast; season. Fold to enclose filling; tie with kitchen string to secure.

3 Cook chicken on heated oiled barbecue until browned and cooked through. Cover chicken; stand 5 minutes then slice thickly.

4 Meanwhile, combine potatoes, garlic, thyme and half the oil in medium bowl. Cook potatoes on heated oiled barbecue until browned lightly.

5 Whisk remaining oil and vinegar in large bowl; add cucumber, onion and remaining spinach, toss gently. Season to taste.

6 Serve chicken with potatoes and spinach salad.

prep + cook time 1 hour
serves 4
nutritional count per serving
12.6g total fat (4g saturated fat); 1810kJ (433 cal); 26.5g carbohydrate; 48.8g protein; 6.5g fibre

PIRI PIRI CHICKEN THIGH FILLETS

4 fresh long red chillies, chopped coarsely
1 teaspoon dried chilli flakes
2 cloves garlic, quartered
1 teaspoon sea salt
2 tablespoons olive oil
1 tablespoon cider vinegar
2 teaspoons brown sugar
8 x 125g chicken thigh fillets

1 Using mortar and pestle, grind fresh chilli, chilli flakes, garlic and salt to make piri piri paste.
2 Combine paste with oil, vinegar, sugar and chicken in medium bowl.
3 Cook chicken on heated oiled barbecue until cooked through. Serve with lime, if desired.

prep + cook time 25 minutes
serves 4
nutritional count per serving
27.2g total fat (6.8g saturated fat); 1822kJ (436 cal); 1.8g carbohydrate; 46.6g protein; 0.3g fibre

CHICKEN SAUSAGES WITH TOMATO SALAD

750g minced chicken
75g drained sun-dried tomatoes
  in oil, chopped finely
1 teaspoon fennel seeds, toasted
6 tablespoons finely chopped
  fresh flat-leaf parsley
1 egg
50g packaged breadcrumbs
90g baby spinach leaves
125g cherry tomatoes, halved
75g green olives
2 teaspoons sherry vinegar
2 teaspoons olive oil

1 Combine mince, tomato, seeds, parsley, egg and breadcrumbs in large bowl. Shape mixture into 12 sausages.
2 Cook sausages on heated oiled barbecue until browned on both sides and cooked through.
3 Meanwhile, combine remaining ingredients in large bowl; season to taste.
4 Serve sausages with salad.

prep + cook time 30 minutes
serves 4
nutritional count per serving
22.6g total fat (5.8g saturated fat); 1885kJ (451 cal); 15.8g carbohydrate; 42.6g protein; 6.1g fibre

tips To toast fennel seeds, place in a small dry frying pan over medium-low heat. Stir 1 minute or until fragrant. You can also use minced turkey for this recipe.

SOY CHICKEN KEBABS WITH ORANGE HOISIN SAUCE

750g chicken breast fillets
2 tablespoons sesame oil
2 tablespoons groundnut oil
2 tablespoons lemon juice
125ml japanese soy sauce
2 garlic cloves, crushed
1 teaspoon chopped fresh
  rosemary

orange hoisin sauce
80ml hoisin sauce
80ml orange juice
1 tablespoon rice vinegar
1 spring onion, finely chopped
2 teaspoons sesame oil

1 Cut chicken into cubes; combine in large bowl with with oils, juice, soy sauce, garlic and rosemary. Cover, refrigerate 2 hours.
2 Thread the chicken onto 12 skewers, reserving marinade. Cook skewers on heated oiled barbecue, basting occasionally with marinade until browned and cooked through.
3 Meanwhile, make hoisin sauce. Serve skewers with dipping sauce.

orange hoisin sauce Combine all the ingredients in a bowl; mix well.

prep + cook time 35 minutes + refrigeration time
makes 12
nutritional count per kebab
8.1g total fat (1.7g saturated fat); 532kJ (127 cal); 2.7g carbohydrate; 10.7g protein; 0.7g fibre
tip You need 12 skewers for this recipe. If using bamboo skewers, soak them in cold water for at least an hour before using to prevent them from splintering and scorching during cooking.

CAJUN CHICKEN BURGERS WITH LEMON YOGURT

2 chicken breast fillets (400g)
2 tablespoons cajun seasoning
4 crusty bread rolls
95g natural yogurt
2 teaspoons finely grated lemon rind
1 medium tomato (150g), chopped finely
1 shallot (25g), chopped finely
½ small ripe avocado (100g), chopped finely
50g mixed salad leaves

1 Cut chicken in half horizontally; sprinkle all over with seasoning. Cook on heated oiled barbecue until brown on both sides and cooked through.

2 Meanwhile, cut rolls in half; toast, cut-sides down, on barbecue.

3 Combine yogurt and rind in small bowl.

4 Combine tomato, shallot and avocado in small bowl; season.

5 Sandwich salad leaves, avocado mixture, chicken and yogurt mixture between rolls.

prep + cook time 30 minutes
serves 4
nutritional count per serving 12.9g total fat (3.3g saturated fat); 1731kJ (414 cal); 41.8g carbohydrate; 30.2g protein; 3.7g fibre
tip For fish burgers, replace the chicken with four firm white fish fillets (125g each).

SPICY YOGURT CHICKEN DRUMSTICKS WITH RAITA

20 chicken drumsticks
180ml natural yogurt
½ teaspoon dried chilli flakes
1 tablespoon ground cumin
1 tablespoon ground coriander
2 teaspoons ground turmeric

raita
6 tablespoons finely chopped
   fresh mint
6 tablespoons finely chopped
   fresh coriander
180ml natural yogurt
1 garlic clove, crushed
1 tablespoon lemon juice

1 Combine drumsticks in large bowl with yogurt, chilli flakes and spices. Cover; refrigerate 30 minutes.
2 Remove drumsticks from marinade; shake off excess. Discard marinade. Cook drumsticks on heated oiled barbecue until cooked through.
3 Meanwhile, make raita. Serve drumsticks with the raita.

raita Combine mint, coriander, yogurt, garlic and juice in small bowl.

prep + cook time 35 minutes + refrigeration time
serves 4
nutritional count per serving
15.4g total fat (6.3g saturated fat); 1509kJ (361 cal); 7.9g carbohydrate; 46.4g protein; 0.6g fibre

HARISSA CHICKEN WITH ORANGE & WATERMELON SALAD

2 medium oranges (480g)

4 chicken thigh cutlets (800g), skin removed

2 tablespoons harissa paste

2 cloves garlic, crushed

1 tablespoon olive oil

750g piece watermelon, sliced thickly

4 tablespoons coarsely chopped fresh mint

35g coarsely chopped roasted unsalted pistachios

200g feta cheese

1 Finely grate 2 teaspoons rind from oranges; segment oranges over small bowl to reserve juice.

2 Combine rind, chicken, paste, garlic and oil in medium bowl; season.

3 Cook chicken on heated oiled barbecue until browned on both sides and cooked through.

4 Meanwhile, combine orange segments, reserved juice, watermelon, mint and nuts in medium bowl; crumble cheese over salad. Serve chicken with salad and lime wedges, if liked.

prep + cook time 45 minutes
serves 4
nutritional count per serving
35.7g total fat (13.3g saturated fat); 2466kJ (590 cal); 16.5g carbohydrate; 49.3g protein; 4.2g fibre

TANDOORI TURKEY WITH PINEAPPLE SALSA

75g tandoori paste
70g natural yogurt
4 x 100g turkey breast steaks
4 medium potatoes (800g),
  unpeeled
1 tablespoon vegetable oil
1 teaspoon brown mustard seeds
1 teaspoon cumin seeds

pineapple salsa
½ small pineapple (450g), sliced
  thickly
1 medium red pepper (200g),
  chopped coarsely
4 tablespoons coarsely chopped
  fresh mint
1 tablespoon lime juice

1 Combine paste, yogurt and turkey steaks in large bowl. Cover; refrigerate 3 hours or overnight.
2 Boil, steam or microwave whole potatoes until tender; drain, cool.
3 Meanwhile, make pineapple salsa.
4 Cut potatoes into 1cm thick slices; combine potatoes, oil and seeds in medium bowl, season. Cook on heated oiled barbecue flat plate until browned lightly.
5 Drain turkey; discard marinade. Cook turkey on heated oiled barbecue until browned on both sides and cooked through.
6 Serve turkey with potatoes and salsa.

pineapple salsa Cook pineapple on heated oiled barbecue until browned lightly; chop coarsely. Combine pineapple with remaining ingredients in medium bowl.

prep + cook time 50 minutes + refrigeration time
serves 4
nutritional count per serving 13.6g total fat (2.2g saturated fat); 1693kJ (405 cal); 35.9g carbohydrate; 29.6g protein; 7.5g fibre

FISH & SEAFOOD

WHOLE FISH & VEGETABLES WITH CHILLI BASIL SAUCE

4 baby cauliflowers (500g), halved
2 trimmed corn cobs (500g), cut into 2cm rounds
400g baby carrots, trimmed
2 tablespoons olive oil
4 x 240g whole white fish

chilli basil sauce
80g butter
2 fresh small red chillies, chopped finely
4 tablespoons fresh basil leaves, shredded finely
1 tablespoon lemon juice

1 Place vegetables and half the oil in large bowl; toss to combine. Cook vegetables on heated oiled barbecue until browned all over and cooked through.
2 Meanwhile, make chilli basil sauce.
3 Score each fish three times both sides; brush all over with remaining oil. Cook fish on heated oiled barbecue until cooked as desired. Serve fish and vegetables drizzled with sauce.

chilli basil sauce Melt butter in small saucepan; add chilli, basil and juice, stir until combined.

prep + cook time 50 minutes
serves 4
nutritional count per serving
32.2g total fat (13.9g saturated fat); 2608kJ (624 cal); 22.7g carbohydrate; 56.4g protein; 9.3g fibre
tip We used whole bream in this recipe, but you can use any whole white fish. Fish fillets can be substituted for the whole fish, if you prefer.

SALMON WITH LIME & CORIANDER PESTO

4 salmon fillets (640g), without skin
90g baby spinach leaves
½ cucumber (130g), cut into thin ribbons
3 red radishes (110g), trimmed, sliced thinly

lime & coriander pesto
50g unsalted roasted cashews
1 fresh small red thai chilli, chopped coarsely
1 large handful fresh coriander leaves
1 large handful fresh mint leaves
1 clove garlic, quartered
2 teaspoons finely grated lime rind
2 tablespoons olive oil
2 tablespoons lime juice
2 tablespoons water

1 Make lime & coriander pesto.
2 Cook fish on heated oiled barbecue until almost cooked through.
3 Meanwhile, combine spinach, cucumber and radish in medium bowl.
4 Serve fish with spinach salad and pesto.

lime & coriander pesto Blend or process nuts, chilli, coriander, mint, garlic and rind until finely chopped. With motor operating, add oil in a thin, steady stream; blend mixture until combined. Stir in juice and the water.

prep + cook time 35 minutes
serves 4
nutritional count per serving
27.4g total fat (5g saturated fat); 1689kJ (404 cal); 3.8g carbohydrate; 34.6g protein; 2.7g fibre

CHILLI MARINATED PRAWNS WITH AÏOLI

24 large uncooked king prawns (1.7kg)
60ml olive oil
3 cloves garlic, crushed
1 tablespoon finely chopped fresh coriander
2 fresh small red thai chillies, chopped finely
1 teaspoon ground cumin
1 teaspoon paprika
1 teaspoon honey
1 tablespoon lime juice
1 cos lettuce, torn
1 cucumber (260g), peeled, halved, sliced thinly
1 medium avocado (250g), chopped coarsely
2 tablespoons olive oil, extra
2 teaspoons lemon juice

aïoli
1 medium garlic bulb (70g)
200g mayonnaise

1 Shell and devein prawns leaving tails intact.
2 Combine prawns, oil, garlic, coriander, chilli, spices, honey and lime juice in medium bowl. Cover, refrigerate 30 minutes.
3 Meanwhile, make aïoli.
4 Remove prawns from marinade; cook on heated oiled barbecue until just cooked through.
5 Combine lettuce, cucumber and avocado in medium bowl; drizzle with combined extra oil and juice. Season to taste.
6 Serve prawns with salad and aïoli.

aïoli Preheat oven to 180°C/160°C fan-assisted. Cut top off garlic bulb. Drizzle bulb with a little olive oil; wrap in foil. Roast in small baking dish, uncovered, about 25 minutes or until tender; cool. Squeeze garlic from each clove; mash to a paste in a small bowl. Mix in mayonnaise and season to taste.

prep + cook time 45 minutes + refrigeration time
serves 6
nutritional count per serving 34g total fat (4.9g saturated fat); 2040kJ (488 cal); 11.5g carbohydrate; 32.4g protein; 4.8g fibre

PRAWN SKEWERS WITH LIME & SPRING ONIONS

36 medium uncooked large
    prawns (1.5kg)
2 tablespoons lime juice
2 tablespoons olive oil
2 cloves garlic, crushed
3 spring onions

1 Peel and devein prawns leaving tails intact.
2 Combine prawns, juice, oil and garlic in large bowl.
3 Cut spring onions into 4cm lengths. Thread three prawns onto each of 12 skewers, threading a piece of spring onion after each prawn.
4 Cook skewers on heated oiled barbecue until browned on both sides and just cooked through. Serve with lime wedges, if liked.

prep + cook time 35 minutes
makes 12
nutritional count per serving
10.4g total fat (1.8g saturated fat); 1078kJ (258 cal); 0.6g carbohydrate; 38.7g protein; 0.4g fibre
tips The prawns can be marinated in lime mixture for up to 1 hour. If you are using metal skewers, oil them first to prevent the prawns sticking. You need 12 skewers for this recipe. If using bamboo skewers, soak them in cold water for at least an hour before using to prevent them from splintering and scorching during cooking.

GRILLED FISH KEBABS

1kg white fish fillets
2 medium courgettes (240g)
1 medium red pepper (200g)
1 medium red onion (170g)
250g natural yogurt
2 tablespoons lemon juice
3 cloves garlic, crushed
2 teaspoons ground cumin
2 teaspoons ground coriander
1 teaspoon sweet paprika
6 tablespoons fresh coriander
   leaves

1 Cut fish, courgettes and pepper into similar-sized chunks; cut onion into wedges. Thread ingredients onto bamboo skewers.
2 Cook skewers on heated oiled barbecue about 10 minutes.
3 Meanwhile, combine yogurt, juice, garlic and spices in small bowl.
4 Serve skewers topped with yogurt mixture; sprinkle with fresh coriander.

prep + cook time 30 minutes
makes 8
nutritional count per kebab
4g total fat (1.6g saturated fat); 706kJ (169 cal); 4.3g carbohydrate; 28.1g protein; 1.3g fibre
tip You need 8 skewers for this recipe. If using bamboo skewers, soak them in cold water for at least an hour before using to prevent them from splintering and scorching during cooking.

FISH FILLETS WITH TOMATO, CAPER & WALNUT DRESSING

4 x 185g white fish fillets

tomato, caper & walnut dressing
250g cherry tomatoes
60g butter
1 tablespoon finely grated
    lemon rind
2 teaspoons lemon juice
1 teaspoon rinsed, drained
    capers, chopped finely
30g finely chopped walnuts
6 tablespoons coarsely chopped
    fresh flat-leaf parsley

1 Make tomato, caper & walnut dressing.
2 Cook fish on heated oiled barbecue until just cooked through. Serve fish with dressing.

tomato, caper & walnut dressing
Cook tomatoes on heated oiled barbecue until tender. Melt butter in small saucepan, add tomatoes and remaining ingredients; stir until hot.

prep + cook time 35 minutes
serves 4
nutritional count per serving
19.8g total fat (9.2g saturated fat); 1471kJ (352 cal); 2g carbohydrate; 40.1g protein; 1.9g fibre
tip You can use any firm white fish fillets you like in this recipe. Check for any small pieces of bone in the fillets and use tweezers to remove them.

FISH WITH FENNEL & LEMON MINT VINAIGRETTE

2 medium fennel bulbs (600g)
1 tablespoon olive oil
2 tablespoons lemon juice
4 tablespoons finely chopped
   fresh mint leaves
1 tablespoon white wine vinegar
4 white fish steaks (750g)

1 Discard stalk from fennel; cut bulb into quarters and remove core.
2 Combine oil, juice, mint and vinegar in small bowl. Brush fennel with some of the vinaigrette. Cook fennel on heated oiled barbecue about 10 minutes, turning often.
3 Meanwhile, brush fish with some of the vinaigrette. Cook on heated oiled barbecue, brushing with more oil mixture during cooking, until just cooked through.
4 Drizzle the fish and fennel with remaining vinaigrette; season. Serve with grilled tomatoes, if you like.

prep + cook time 25 minutes
serves 4
nutritional count per serving
8.8g total fat (2g saturated fat); 1074kJ (257 cal); 3.2g carbohydrate; 39.3g protein; 2.7g fibre
tip We used swordfish steaks, but any firm white fish will be fine.

THAI FISH CAKE SKEWERS

1kg boneless white fish fillets
2 tablespoons red curry paste
1 egg
2 shallots (50g) chopped finely
2 tablespoons finely chopped
  fresh coriander
2 fresh small red chillies, sliced
  thinly
2 teaspoons finely grated lime
  rind
2 tablespoons lime juice

1 Blend or process fish, paste and egg until combined. Transfer mixture to large bowl, mix in shallot, coriander, chilli, rind and juice; season.
2 Roll rounded tablespoons of mixture into balls. Thread 3 balls onto each skewer.
3 Cook fish cakes, flattening slightly, on heated oiled barbecue until browned on both sides and cooked through. Serve skewers with lime wedges and sweet chilli sauce, if liked.

prep + cook time 35 minutes
makes 8
nutritional count per skewer
7.4g total fat (1.8g saturated fat); 911kJ (218 cal); 1g carbohydrate; 35.9g protein; 1g fibre
tips The fish cake mixture can be covered and refrigerated for 2 hours or overnight before cooking. You need 8 skewers for this recipe. If using bamboo skewers, soak them in cold water for at least an hour before using to prevent them from splintering and scorching during cooking.

VEGETARIAN

MEXICAN VEGETABLE SKEWERS

2 corn cobs, trimmed
1 medium green pepper (200g)
1 small red onion (80g)
250g cherry tomatoes on the vine
35g packet taco seasoning
2 tablespoons bottled chunky
   tomato salsa

1 Thickly slice corn cobs. Coarsely chop pepper; cut onion into 8 wedges. Combine corn, pepper, onion and tomatoes with taco seasoning and salsa in large bowl; season.

2 Thread vegetables onto metal skewers; cook skewers on heated oiled barbecue about 15 minutes.

3 Serve skewers with extra tomato salsa, soured cream and tortillas, if liked.

prep + cook time 35 minutes
makes 8
nutritional count per skewer
9g total fat (0.3g saturated fat); 978kJ (234 cal); 37g carbohydrate; 9.1g protein; 10.6g fibre
tip You need 8 skewers for this recipe. We used metal skewers to pierce through the hard core of the corn slices.

MUSHROOMS WITH HERB BUTTER

80g butter, melted
1 teaspoon grated lime rind
1 tablespoon lime juice
1 tablespoon finely chopped
   fresh flat-leaf parsley
1 tablespoon finely chopped
   fresh basil
6 large flat mushrooms (840g)

1 Combine butter, rind, juice and herbs in small bowl.

2 Cook mushrooms on heated oiled barbecue, brushing with half the butter mixture, until mushrooms are just tender and browned. Serve with remaining butter.

prep + cook time 20 minutes
serves 6
nutritional count per serving
11.4g total fat (7.2g saturated fat); 548kJ (131 cal); 0.6g carbohydrate; 5.2g protein; 3.6g fibre

HALOUMI, ASPARAGUS & RED ONION SKEWERS

125ml balsamic vinegar
1 tablespoon honey
1 tablespoon light brown sugar
350g haloumi cheese
150g asparagus
1 small red onion (80g)

1 Combine vinegar, honey and sugar in small saucepan; stir over low heat, without boiling, until sugar dissolves. Bring to the boil; boil, uncovered, about 5 minutes or until syrup thickens slightly, cool.

2 Meanwhile, cut cheese and asparagus into 2.5cm pieces; cut onion into thin wedges. Thread cheese, asparagus and onion onto bamboo skewers; season.

3 Cook skewers on heated oiled barbecue until browned and tender. Serve skewers immediately, drizzled with balsamic syrup.

prep + cook time 35 minutes
makes 8
nutritional count per skewer
7.8g total fat (4.8g saturated fat); 564kJ (135 cal); 6.1g carbohydrate; 9.8g protein; 0.4g fibre

tips Thick asparagus is best for this recipe. You need 8 skewers for this recipe. If using bamboo skewers, soak them in cold water for at least an hour before using to prevent them from splintering and scorching during cooking.

MEDITERRANEAN VEGETABLES WITH OREGANO DRESSING

1 medium red pepper (200g)
1 medium yellow pepper (200g)
1 large red onion (300g), halved, cut into wedges
1 small sweet potato (250g), sliced thinly lengthways
2 baby aubergines (120g), sliced thinly lengthways
2 medium courgettes (240g), halved lengthways
340g jar artichoke hearts, drained, halved
100g pitted kalamata olives
1 small radicchio (150g), trimmed, leaves separated

oregano dressing
60ml olive oil
2 tablespoons red wine vinegar
2 tablespoons lemon juice
2 cloves garlic, crushed
1 tablespoon finely chopped fresh oregano leaves

1 Make oregano dressing.
2 Quarter peppers, discard seeds and membranes; cut flesh into thick strips.
3 Cook pepper on heated oiled barbecue until tender. Cook onion, sweet potato, aubergine, courgette and artichoke, in batches, on heated oiled barbecue until tender.
4 Combine char-grilled vegetables, olives and dressing in large bowl; toss gently. Serve with radicchio.

oregano dressing Combine ingredients in screw-top jar; shake well.

prep + cook time 55 minutes
serves 4
nutritional count per serving
14.8g total fat (2g saturated fat); 1104kJ (264 cal); 22.8g carbohydrate; 6.4g protein; 7.6g fibre
tip Radicchio is also called red chicory. You can use ordinary chicory if you can't find red.

TOFU AND VEGGIE BURGERS

300g firm silken tofu
1 tablespoon olive oil
1 medium brown onion (150g),
 chopped finely
2 cloves garlic, crushed
¼ teaspoon sweet paprika
1 teaspoon ground turmeric
2 teaspoons ground coriander
1 small courgette (90g), grated
 coarsely
140g fresh breadcrumbs
190g hummus
70g greek-style yogurt
1 large loaf ciabatta
4 tablespoons coarsely chopped
 fresh mint
6 tablespoons coarsely chopped
 fresh flat-leaf parsley
1 spring onion, sliced thinly
30g pea shoots, trimmed

1 Pat tofu dry with absorbent paper. Spread tofu, in single layer, on absorbent-paper-lined tray; cover tofu with more paper, stand 20 minutes.

2 Meanwhile, heat oil in medium frying pan; cook brown onion and garlic, stirring, until onion softens. Add spices; cook, stirring, until fragrant.

3 Combine onion mixture in large bowl with tofu, courgette and breadcrumbs; shape into four patties. Cover; refrigerate 30 minutes.

4 Meanwhile, combine hummus and yogurt in small bowl.

5 Cut bread into four pieces. Split each piece in half horizontally; toast cut sides on heated oiled barbecue.

6 Cook patties on same oiled barbecue until browned both sides and hot.

7 Spread bread with hummus mixture; sandwich combined mint, parsley and spring onion, patties and shoots between bread pieces.

prep + cook time 40 minutes + standing and refrigeration time
serves 4
nutritional count per serving
24.1g total fat (4.6g saturated fat); 2880kJ (689 cal); 81.5g carbohydrate; 30.2g protein; 11.7g fibre

FELAFEL BURGERS

625g canned chickpeas, rinsed, drained
1 medium brown onion (150g), chopped coarsely
2 cloves garlic, quartered
6 tablespoons chopped fresh flat-leaf parsley
2 teaspoons ground coriander
1 teaspoon ground cumin
1 teaspoon bicarbonate of soda
2 tablespoons plain flour
1 egg
1 large loaf ciabatta
1 large tomato (220g), sliced thinly
20g rocket

yogurt & tahini sauce
70g natural yogurt
2 tablespoons tahini
1 tablespoon lemon juice

1 Blend or process chickpeas, onion, garlic, parsley, coriander, cumin, bicarbonate of soda, flour and egg until almost smooth. Shape mixture into four patties. Cook patties on heated oiled barbecue about 10 minutes or until browned both sides.
2 Cut bread into quarters; toast both sides on heated oiled barbecue.
3 Meanwhile, make yogurt & tahini sauce.
4 Split each piece of bread in half horizontally; sandwich sauce, tomato, patties and rocket between bread halves.

yogurt & tahini sauce Combine ingredients in small bowl.

prep + cook time 25 minutes
serves 4
nutritional count per serving
13.9g total fat (2.4g saturated fat); 2195kJ (525 cal); 71.2g carbohydrate; 22.6g protein; 10.9g fibre
tip When cooking the felafel, use two spatulas to turn them carefully, so they don't break.

SALADS &
ACCOMPANIMENTS

GREEK SALAD

4 medium plum tomatoes (300g),
  sliced thinly
1 cucumber (260g), chopped
  coarsely
1 small red onion (80g), sliced
  thinly
75g pitted kalamata olives
150g feta cheese, chopped
  coarsely
2 tablespoons olive oil
2 tablespoons lemon juice
2 teaspoons fresh oregano leaves

1 Combine tomato, cucumber, onion, olives and cheese in large bowl.
2 Place remaining ingredients in screw-top jar; shake well. Drizzle dressing over salad.

prep time 15 minutes
serves 4
nutritional count per serving
18.2g total fat (7.1g saturated fat); 991kJ (237 cal); 9g carbohydrate; 8.3g protein; 2.4g fibre

ITALIAN BROWN RICE SALAD

750ml vegetable stock
2 teaspoons olive oil
1 small brown onion (80g),
   chopped finely
300g brown medium-grain rice
1 teaspoon finely grated lime rind
1 clove garlic, crushed
45g roasted slivered almonds
100g sun-dried tomatoes,
   chopped coarsely
60g pitted black olives, chopped
   coarsely
6 tablespoons coarsely chopped
   fresh basil
3 tablespoons coarsely chopped
   fresh flat-leaf parsley

lime & mustard dressing
2 tablespoons lime juice
2 tablespoons white wine vinegar
2 cloves garlic, crushed
2 teaspoons dijon mustard

1 Place stock in medium saucepan; bring to the boil. Reduce heat; simmer, covered.
2 Meanwhile, heat oil in large saucepan; cook onion, stirring, until soft. Add rice, rind and garlic; stir to coat rice in onion mixture.
3 Add stock; bring to the boil. Reduce heat; simmer, covered, about 50 minutes or until rice is tender and liquid is absorbed.
4 Place ingredients for lime & mustard dressing in screw-top jar; shake well.
5 Add remaining ingredients and dressing to rice mixture in pan; toss gently to combine.
6 Serve salad warm; top with fresh flat-leaf parsley, if you like.

prep + cook time 1 hour 15 minutes
serves 4
nutritional count per serving
13.3 g total fat (1.8g saturated fat); 1923kJ (460 cal); 76.3g carbohydrate; 14.7g protein; 9.4g fibre

COUSCOUS SALAD WITH CHICKPEAS

300g couscous
375ml boiling water
20g butter
400g can chickpeas, rinsed,
  drained
55g sultanas
50g roasted pine nuts
100g rocket, chopped coarsely
1 large handful finely chopped
  fresh flat-leaf parsley
120g pitted green olives

preserved lemon dressing
1 tablespoon finely grated lemon
  rind
60ml lemon juice
60ml olive oil
2 tablespoons rinsed and drained
  finely chopped preserved
  lemon

1 Combine couscous with the water in large heatproof bowl, cover; stand about 5 minutes or until water is absorbed, fluffing with fork occasionally. Stir in butter. Stand 10 minutes.
2 Place ingredients for preserved lemon dressing in screw-top jar; shake well.
3 Place couscous in large bowl with remaining ingredients and dressing; toss gently to combine.

prep time 20 minutes
serves 4
nutritional count per serving
29g total fat (5.5g saturated fat); 268kJ (686 cal); 85.6g carbohydrate; 17.2g protein; 6.5g fibre

BEAN SALAD WITH CREAMY DRESSING

400g can butter beans, rinsed,
  drained
400g can borlotti beans, rinsed,
  drained
250g cherry tomatoes, quartered
12 mini mozzarella balls (180g),
  halved
60g rocket
80g roasted pine nuts

creamy dressing
2 tablespoons olive oil
2 tablespoons white wine vinegar
2 teaspoons white balsamic
  vinegar
2 tablespoons coarsely chopped
  fresh basil leaves
60ml single cream

1 Make creamy dressing.
2 Place beans in large bowl
with remaining ingredients and
dressing; stir gently to combine.

creamy dressing Combine oil,
vinegars and basil in small bowl.
Add cream; whisk until combined.

prep time 15 minutes
serves 4
nutritional count per serving
37.1g total fat (11g saturated fat);
1944kJ (465 cal); 13g carbohydrate;
17.1g protein; 7.7g fibre

CHARRED PEAR, CELERY & WALNUT SALAD WITH TARRAGON PESTO

2 stalks celery (300g), trimmed
4 small rocha pears (400g), sliced
  thinly lengthways
1 small red pepper (150g),
  deseeded, chopped finely
1 large handful fresh celery leaves
50g walnuts, roasted, chopped
  coarsely

tarragon pesto
1 large handful fresh tarragon
  leaves
2 slices white bread, crusts
  removed
60ml milk
60ml water
2 tablespoons olive oil
1 teaspoon sea salt

1 Make tarragon pesto.
2 Cut celery into 8cm pieces; cut pieces lengthways into matchstick-sized pieces.
3 Cook pear on heated oiled barbecue until browned lightly both sides.
4 Combine celery, pear, pepper, celery leaves, nuts and 60ml of the tarragon pesto in large bowl; season to taste.
5 Serve salad drizzled with remaining pesto.

tarragon pesto Blend or process ingredients until smooth.

prep + cook time 30 minutes
serves 4
nutritional count per serving
18.9g total fat (2.3g saturated fat); 1162kJ (278 cal); 21.1g carbohydrate; 4.7g protein; 5.2g fibre
tips Use the yellow and lighter green leaves from the heart of the celery. Add sliced blue cheese or brie to the salad, if you like.

CARAMELISED FIG, ORANGE & FENNEL SALAD

6 medium figs (360g), halved
1 medium fennel bulb (300g),
  trimmed
90g mixed salad leaves
2 large oranges (300g),
  segmented

orange & honey dressing
1 teaspoon finely grated orange
  rind
2 tablespoons orange juice
1 tablespoon honey
1 tablespoon olive oil

1 Make orange & honey dressing.
2 Place figs and dressing in large bowl; turn gently to coat. Remove figs from dressing; reserve dressing.
3 Cook figs on heated oiled barbecue until caramelised.
4 Using a mandolin, V-slicer or sharp knife, slice fennel thinly. Add salad leaves, fennel and orange to bowl with dressing; toss gently to combine. Place salad on serving platter; top with figs.

orange & honey dressing
Combine ingredients in screw-top jar; shake well, season to taste.

prep + cook time 25 minutes
serves 4
nutritional count per serving
4.9g total fat (0.6g saturated fat); 594kJ (142 cal); 19.9g carbohydrate; 2.5g protein; 4.8g fibre

GARLIC BREAD

1 large loaf ciabatta
50g butter, melted
2 cloves garlic, crushed
2 tablespoons finely chopped
fresh flat-leaf parsley

1 Halve bread horizontally; cut each half into four pieces.
2 Combine butter, garlic and parsley in small bowl; brush over bread pieces.
3 Cook bread on heated oiled barbecue until browned both sides.

prep + cook time 10 minutes
serves 4
nutritional count per serving
11.2g total fat (5.9g saturated fat); 1229kJ (294 cal); 38.9g carbohydrate; 7.9g protein; 2.6g fibre

ASPARAGUS WITH THREE TOPPINGS

600g asparagus, trimmed

anchovies & garlic
2 tablespoons olive oil
1 clove garlic, sliced thinly
3 drained anchovies, chopped
   coarsely

parmesan butter
25g butter
2 tablespoons parmesan cheese
   flakes

balsamic dressing
2 tablespoons olive oil
3 teaspoons balsamic vinegar
1 medium tomato (150g), peeled,
   deseeded, chopped finely
1 tablespoon small basil leaves

1 Cook asparagus on heated
oiled barbecue about 5 minutes
or until tender.
2 Make toppings.
3 Arrange asparagus in three
piles on serving platter. Top each
pile with one of the following
toppings.

anchovies & garlic Heat oil in
small frying pan; cook garlic and
anchovy until browned lightly.
Sprinkle over asparagus.

nutritional count per serving
18.8g total fat (2.7g saturated fat);
786kJ (188 cal); 1.6g carbohydrate;
3.8g protein; 1.8g fibre

parmesan butter Melt butter
in small saucepan. Pour over
asparagus; sprinkle with cheese.

nutritional count per serving
10.6g total fat (6.9g saturated fat);
506kJ (121 cal); 1.5g carbohydrate;
5.2g protein; 1.5g fibre

balsamic dressing Combine
ingredients in small bowl. Spoon
over asparagus.

nutritional count per serving
18.4g total fat (2.6g saturated fat);
790kJ (189 cal); 2.8g carbohydrate;
3.3g protein; 2.5g fibre

prep + cook time 20 minutes
serves 4

BARBECUED CORN ON THE COB WITH TAHINI

4 whole corn cobs
45g butter, softened
1½ tablespoons tahini
½ teaspoon cayenne pepper
2 teaspoons finely chopped
   fresh coriander

1 Remove silk from corn cobs, leaving husks intact. Soak corn cobs in water for 15 minutes.
2 Meanwhile, combine butter, tahini, cayenne pepper and coriander in small bowl. Peel back corn husks carefully; brush butter mixture all over corn then carefully fold husks back over corn. Tie tops with string or secure with small piece of foil.
3 Cook corn on heated barbecue about 15 minutes, turning regularly to cook evenly. Peel husks from corn, cut cobs in half before serving.

prep + cook time 40 minutes
serves 8
nutritional count per serving
8.6g total fat (3.5g saturated fat); 903kJ (216 cal); 24g carbohydrate; 6.9g protein; 7.1g fibre

BARBECUED ROSEMARY POTATO SKINS

5 medium potatoes (1kg)
2 tablespoons olive oil
2 teaspoons fine sea salt
1 teaspoon seasoned pepper
2 teaspoons finely chopped
  fresh rosemary
300g soured cream

1 Scrub potatoes well; brush with half of the oil. Cook in covered barbecue, using indirect heat, following manufacturer's instructions, about 50 minutes or until tender; cool.
2 Cut each potato into six wedges; carefully scoop out flesh, leaving skins intact (reserve potato flesh for another use).
3 Place potato skins, skin-side up, in single layer on wire rack over disposable baking dish. Brush with remaining oil; sprinkle with combined salt, pepper and rosemary.
4 Cook in covered barbecue, using indirect heat, about 30 minutes or until crisp.
5 Serve hot with soured cream.

prep + cook time 1 hour 35 minutes + cooling time
serves 4
nutritional count per serving
38.3g total fat (21g saturated fat); 1937kJ (463 cal); 21.7g carbohydrate; 4.8g protein; 3.3g fibre

SAUCES, SALSAS & MARINADES

FOUR SUPER SALAD DRESSINGS

CLASSIC FRENCH DRESSING

Place 60ml white vinegar, 180ml olive oil, ½ teaspoon granulated sugar and 1 teaspoon dijon mustard in a screw-top jar; shake well.

prep time 5 minutes
makes about 250ml
nutritional count per tablespoon
13.7g total fat (1.9g saturated fat); 506kJ (121 cal); 0.2g carbohydrate; 0g protein; 0g fibre

SESAME SOY DRESSING

Combine 1 tablespoon toasted sesame seeds, 1 tablespoon sesame oil, 2 finely chopped shallots (50g), 1 tablespoon kecap manis and 60ml lime juice in a small bowl.

prep time 5 minutes
makes 125ml
nutritional count per tablespoon
1.4g total fat (0.2g saturated fat); 63kJ (15 cal); 0.2g carbohydrate; 0.3g protein; 0.1g fibre

BALSAMIC & GARLIC DRESSING

Whisk 2 tablespoons balsamic vinegar, 60ml lemon juice, 1 crushed clove garlic and 180ml olive oil in a small bowl until combined.

prep time 5 minutes
makes 310ml
nutritional count per tablespoon
10.9g total fat (1.5g saturated fat); 406kJ (97 cal); 0.1g carbohydrate; 0g protein; 0g fibre

CLASSIC ITALIAN DRESSING

Place 2 tablespoons white wine vinegar, 2 tablespoons lemon juice, ½ teaspoon granulated sugar, 2 crushed cloves garlic, 180ml olive oil, 1 tablespoon finely chopped fresh basil leaves and 1 tablespoon finely chopped fresh oregano leaves in a screw-top jar; shake well.

prep time 5 minutes
makes about 250ml
nutritional count per tablespoon
13.7g total fat (1.9g saturated fat); 510kJ (122 cal); 0.3g carbohydrate; 0.1g protein; 0.1g fibre

clockwise from top left: Classic French dressing, Sesame soy dressing, Classic Italian dressing, Balsamic & garlic dressing

FOUR MARVELLOUS MARINADES

BALSAMIC VINEGAR MARINADE

Combine 60ml lemon juice, 2 tablespoons olive oil, 60ml balsamic vinegar, 2 crushed cloves garlic, 3 teaspoons brown sugar and 2 teaspoons finely chopped thyme in a medium jug.

prep time 5 minutes
makes 180ml
nutritional count per quantity
36.7g total fat (5.9g saturated fat); 1643kJ (393 cal); 11.6g carbohydrate; 1g protein; 1.5g fibre

RED WINE MARINADE

Combine 125ml dry red wine, 2 teaspoons dijon mustard, 1 crushed clove garlic and ½ teaspoon finely chopped thyme in a medium jug.

prep time 5 minutes
makes 125ml
nutritional count per quantity
0.3g total fat (0.04g saturated fat); 382kJ (91 cal); 1.1g carbohydrate; 1.3g protein; 1.1g fibre

YOGURT MARINADE

Combine 140g natural yogurt, 1 crushed clove garlic, 1 fresh red chilli, deseeded and finely chopped, ½ teaspoon sweet paprika and 2 teaspoons finely chopped fresh mint in a small bowl.

prep time 5 minutes
makes 125ml
nutritional count per quantity
5g total fat (3.5g saturated fat); 528kJ (126 cal); 13g carbohydrate; 4.9g protein; 1.2g fibre

HONEY SOY MARINADE

Combine 1 tablespoon warmed honey, 80ml soy sauce, 1 teaspoon sesame oil, 2 crushed cloves garlic and 2 teaspoons grated fresh ginger in a small jug.

prep time 5 minutes
makes 125ml
nutritional count per quantity
4.8g total fat (0.7g saturated fat); 170kJ (170cal); 26.6g carbohydrate; 5g protein; 1.2g fibre

clockwise from top left: Balsamic vinegar marinade, Honey soy marinade, Red wine marinade, Yogurt marinade

FOUR BRILLIANT BURGER SAUCES

MAYONNAISE

Combine 2 egg yolks, ½ teaspoon salt and ¾ teaspoon mustard powder in medium bowl. Gradually add 165ml light olive oil and 80ml olive oil, in thin, steady stream, whisking constantly until mixture thickens. Stir 1 tablespoon white vinegar into mayonnaise.

prep + cook time 15 minutes
makes 250ml
nutritional count per tablespoon
19.1g total fat (2.8g saturated fat); 715kJ (171 cal); 0.0g carbohydrate; 0.5g protein; 0.0g fibre

SWEET CHILLI SAUCE

Combine 6 finely chopped fresh long red chillies, 250ml white vinegar and 220g caster sugar in small saucepan; stir over heat, without boiling, until sugar dissolves. Simmer, uncovered, 15 minutes. Add 2 crushed garlic cloves; simmer, uncovered, about 15 minutes or until mixture reduces by half. Cool.

prep + cook time 55 minutes
+ cooling time
makes 250ml
nutritional count per tablespoon
0.1g total fat (0.0g saturated fat); 309kJ (74 cal); 18.4g carbohydrate; 0.1g protein; 0.1g fibre

TANGY BARBECUE SAUCE

Combine 250ml tomato ketchup, 125ml apple cider vinegar, 60ml worcestershire sauce, 150g dark brown sugar, 2 tablespoons american-style mustard, 1 finely chopped fresh small red chilli, 1 crushed clove garlic and 1 tablespoon lemon juice in medium saucepan; bring to a boil then reduce heat. Simmer, uncovered, stirring occasionally, 20 minutes.

prep + cook time 30 minutes
makes 500ml
nutritional count per tablespoon
0.1g total fat (0.0g saturated fat); 163kJ (39 cal); 9.3g carbohydrate; 0.3g protein; 0.3g fibre

TOMATO KETCHUP

Heat 1 tablespoon olive oil in large saucepan; cook 1 coarsely chopped large brown onion (300g), stirring, until soft. Add 2 tablespoons dark brown sugar, 3 x 400g cans chopped tomatoes, ¼ teaspoon ground allspice and ½ teaspoon celery salt; bring to a boil then reduce heat. Simmer, uncovered, stirring occasionally, for 30 minutes or until mixture thickens. Stir in 2 tablespoons tomato paste and 80ml white vinegar; cook, uncovered, 5 minutes. Blend or process sauce until smooth; push through fine sieve into medium bowl. Discard solids. Serve cold.

prep + cook time 50 minutes
+ cooling time
makes 875ml
nutritional count per tablespoon
0.5g total fat (0.1g saturated fat); 63kJ (15 cal); 1.9g carbohydrate; 0.3g protein, 0.5g fibre

clockwise from top left:
Mayonnaise, Sweet chilli sauce, Tomato ketchup, Tangy barbecue sauce

FOUR SIZZLING SALSAS

BLACK BEAN SALSA

In a large bowl combine 400g canned black beans, rinsed and drained, with 2 medium red peppers (400g), roasted, peeled and thinly sliced, 270g frozen corn kernels, 1 small chopped red onion (80g), 1 finely chopped fresh red chilli, 4 tablespoons coarsely chopped coriander, 2 crushed cloves garlic, 2 tablespoons olive oil, 1 tablespoon finely grated lime rind, 125ml lime juice and 1 teaspoon ground cumin.

prep time 10 minutes
makes 1 litre
nutritional count per tablespoon
0.9g total fat (0.1g saturated fat); 84kJ (20 cal); 2g carbohydrate; 0.7g protein; 0.7g fibre

clockwise from top left: Black bean salsa, Mango & avocado salsa, Roasted pepper & green olive salsa, Salsa fresca

MANGO & AVOCADO SALSA

Combine 1 coarsely chopped mango (430g), 1 large coarsely chopped avocado (320g), 1 finely chopped small red onion (80g), 1 finely chopped small red pepper (150g), 1 finely chopped small fresh red chilli, and 2 tablespoons lime juice together in a medium bowl.

prep time 10 minutes
makes 625ml
nutritional count per tablespoon
1.7g total fat (0.4g saturated fat); 100kJ (24 cal); 1.6g carbohydrate; 0.4g protein; 0.4g fibre

SALSA FRESCA

Combine 6 tablespoons finely chopped flat-leaf parsley, 3 tablespoons finely chopped fresh dill, 3 tablespoons finely chopped fresh chives, 1 tablespoon wholegrain mustard, 2 tablespoons lemon juice, 2 tablespoons finely chopped drained, rinsed baby capers, 1 crushed clove garlic, 80ml olive oil together in a small bowl.

prep time 10 minutes
makes 250ml
nutritional count per tablespoon
6.1g total fat (1g saturated fat); 242kJ (58 cal); 0.5g carbohydrate; 0.3g protein; 0.6g fibre

ROASTED PEPPER & GREEN OLIVE SALSA

Blend or process 120g pitted, chopped green olives until smooth. Stir in 150g roasted red pepper, 1 small finely chopped red onion (80g), 1 tablespoon lime juice, 4 tablespoons coarsely chopped fresh coriander and a further 120g pitted, chopped green olives.

prep time 10 minutes
makes 500ml
nutritional count per tablespoon
2.6g total fat (0.3g saturated fat); 102kJ (24 cal); 0.7g carbohydrate; 0.4g protein; 0.6g fibre

GLOSSARY

allspice also known as pimento or Jamaican pepper; available whole or ground.

bicarbonate of soda also called baking soda; primarily used in cooking, as a leavening agent.

bread

ciabatta meaning 'slipper' in Italian, which is the traditional shape of this popular crisp-crusted white bread.

sourdough so-named, not because of its sour taste, but because it's made by using a small amount of 'starter dough', which contains a yeast culture mixed into flour and water. Part of the resulting dough is then saved to use as the starter dough for the next batch of bread.

capers the grey-green buds of a warm climate shrub sold either dried and salted or pickled in vinegar brine.

cayenne pepper thin-fleshed, long, very-hot red chilli; usually purchased dried and ground.

cheese

feta a crumbly textured goat's- or sheep's-milk cheese with a sharp, salty taste.

haloumi a firm, cream-coloured sheep's milk cheese matured in brine; can be grilled or fried, briefly, without breaking down.

mozzarella a semi-soft cheese with a delicate, fresh taste; has a low melting point and stringy texture when hot.

parmesan a sharp-tasting, dry, hard cheese, made from skimmed or semi-skimmed milk and aged for at least a year.

cumin available both ground and as whole seeds; cumin has a warm, earthy, rather strong flavour.

fennel bulb vegetable, also known as finocchio or anise. Also the name given to dried seeds that have a distinct liquorice flavour.

five-spice powder a fragrant mixture of ground cinnamon, cloves, star anise, sichuan pepper and fennel seeds.

harissa a North African paste made from dried red chillies, garlic, olive oil and caraway seeds. It can be used as a rub for meat, an ingredient in sauces and dressings, or eaten on its own as a condiment.

hoisin sauce a thick, sweet and spicy Chinese paste made from salted fermented soy beans, onions and garlic.

lemongrass a tall, clumping, lemon-smelling and -tasting, sharp edged grass; use only the white lower part of each stem.

kecap manis also known as kicap manis and ketjap manis; an Indonesian sweet, thick soy sauce which has sugar and spices added.

maple syrup distilled from the sap of maple trees found only in Canada and parts of North America. Maple-flavoured syrup is not an adequate substitute for the real thing.

mirin sweet low-alcohol rice wine used in Japanese cooking.

mustard

american-style a mild mustard which is sweet in flavour.

powder finely ground yellow (white) mustard seeds.

wholegrain also known as seeded mustard. A French-style coarse-grain mustard made from crushed mustard seeds and Dijon-style French mustard.

olives

black harvested when ripe, black olives are mostly used in cooking, on pizzas and in salads.

green harvested before fully ripened, green olives are, as a rule, denser and more bitter than their black or brown relatives.

kalamata small, sharp-tasting brine-cured black olives.

palm sugar also called nam tan pip, jaggery, jawa or gula melaka; made from the sap of the sugar palm tree. Light brown to black in colour; sold in rock-hard cakes or granulated. If unavailable, use brown sugar. Available from some supermarkets and Asian food stores.

paprika ground dried red pepper; available sweet, smoked or hot.

pine nuts also known as pignoli; small, cream-coloured kernels obtained from the cones of different varieties of pine trees.

preserved lemon a North African specialty, the citrus is preserved, usually whole, in a mixture of salt and lemon juice or oil. To use, remove and discard pulp, squeeze juice from rind, then rinse rind well before slicing thinly.

prosciutto salted-cured, air-dried (unsmoked), pressed ham; usually sold in paper-thin slices, ready to eat.

sake Japan's favourite rice wine, sake is used in cooking, marinating and as part of dipping sauces. If unavailable, dry sherry, vermouth or brandy can be used as a substitute. When consumed as a drink, it can be served cold or warm.

sesame oil made from roasted, crushed, white sesame seeds; a flavouring rather than a cooking medium.

soy sauce made from fermented soy beans; several variations are available.

Japanese soy sauce an all-purpose low-sodium sauce made with more wheat content than its Chinese counterparts. Possibly the best table soy and the one to choose if you only want one variety.

tahini paste made from crushed sesame seeds.

tofu also known as bean curd, tofu is an off-white, custard-like product made from the 'milk' of crushed soy beans. It comes fresh as soft or firm, and processed as fried or pressed dried sheets. Leftover fresh tofu can be refrigerated in water (which is changed daily) up to four days. Silken tofu refers to the method by which it is made – where it is strained through silk.

vinegar

balsamic authentic only when from the province of Modena, Italy, balsamic vinegar is made from a regional wine of white trebbiano grapes specially processed then aged in antique wooden casks to give the exquisite pungent flavour.

cider made from fermented apples.

rice based on fermented rice.

sherry mellow wine vinegar named for its colour.

white made from spirit of cane sugar.

wine based on fermented red or white wine.

worcestershire sauce a thin, dark-brown, spicy sauce used as seasoning for meat and gravies, and as a condiment.

INDEX

CONVERSION CHARTS

measures

One metric tablespoon holds 20ml; one metric teaspoon holds 5ml.

All cup and spoon measurements are level. The most accurate way of measuring dry ingredients is to weigh them. When measuring liquids, use a clear glass or plastic jug with metric markings.

We use large eggs with an average weight of 60g.

dry measures

METRIC	IMPERIAL
15g	½oz
30g	1oz
60g	2oz
90g	3oz
125g	4oz (¼lb)
155g	5oz
185g	6oz
220g	7oz
250g	8oz (½lb)
280g	9oz
315g	10oz
345g	11oz
375g	12oz (¾lb)
410g	13oz
440g	14oz
470g	15oz
500g	16oz (1lb)
750g	24oz (1½lb)
1kg	32oz (2lb)

liquid measures

METRIC	IMPERIAL
30ml	1 fluid oz
60ml	2 fluid oz
100ml	3 fluid oz
125ml	4 fluid oz
150ml	5 fluid oz
190ml	6 fluid oz
250ml	8 fluid oz
300ml	10 fluid oz
500ml	16 fluid oz
600ml	20 fluid oz
1000ml (1 litre)	32 fluid oz

length measures

3mm	⅛in
6mm	¼in
1cm	½in
2cm	¾in
2.5cm	1in
5cm	2in
6cm	2½in
8cm	3in
10cm	4in
13cm	5in
15cm	6in
18cm	7in
20cm	8in
23cm	9in
25cm	10in
28cm	11in
30cm	12in (1ft)

oven temperatures

These are fan-assisted temperatures. If you have a conventional oven (ie. not fan-assisted), increase temperatures by 10–20°.

	°C (CELSIUS)	°F (FAHRENHEIT)	GAS MARK
Very low	100	210	½
Low	130	260	1–2
Moderately low	140	280	3
Moderate	160	325	4–5
Moderately hot	180	350	6
Hot	200	400	7–8
Very hot	220	425	9